Adventures in Canadian History

THE RAILWAY PATHFINDERS

PIERRE BERTON

THE RAILWAY PATHFINDERS

ILLUSTRATIONS BY PAUL MCCUSKER

An M&S Paperback Original from
McClelland & Stewart Inc.
The Canadian Publishers

An M&S Paperback Original from McClelland & Stewart Inc.

First printing March 1992

Canadian Cataloguing in Publication Data

Berton, Pierre, 1920-
The railway pathfinders

(Adventures in Canadian history. Canada moves west)
"An M&S paperback original."
Includes index.
ISBN 0-7710-1437-6

1. Canadian Pacific Railway Company – History – Juvenile literature.
2. Canadian Pacific Railway Company – Biography – Juvenile literature.
3. Railroads – Canada – Surveying – History – 19th century – Juvenile
literature. 4. Northwest, Canadian – Discovery and exploration – Juvenile
literature. 5. Surveyors – Canada – Biography – Juvenile literature. I. Title.
II. Series: Berton, Pierre, 1920-   . Adventures in Canadian history. Canada
moves west.

HE2810.C3B4 1992   j385'.0971   C92-093664-4

Series design by Tania Craan
Original text design by Martin Gould
Cover illustration by Scott Cameron
Interior illustrations by Paul McCusker
Maps by James Loates
Editor: Peter Carver

Typesetting by M&S

Printed and bound in Canada

McClelland & Stewart Inc.
The Canadian Publishers
481 University Avenue
Toronto, Ontario
M5G 2E9

Contents

Maps appear on page 10 and page 36

Adventures in Canadian History

THE RAILWAY PATHFINDERS

OVERVIEW

The ties that bind

THE STORY OF THE BUILDING of the Pacific Railway across the gnarled rocks of the Canadian Shield, across the waving buffalo grass of the central plains, and through the passes of three mountain ranges in British Columbia, is one of the great epics in Canadian history.

The railway held us together in the days before automobiles, buses, airplanes or broadcasting. Before it was built Canada was not a transcontinental country. One thousand miles (1,600 km) of rock and muskeg separated Ottawa and Toronto from the West. The prairies were the preserve of the Hudson's Bay Company, and of the Indians and Métis. There weren't even bridges across the great rivers because the Hudson's Bay Company didn't want settlers to invade their private territory.

Beyond the plains stood a wall of cloud-tossed peaks – no fewer than three great mountain ramparts, the Rockies, the Selkirks, and the Coastal Mountains.

Vancouver did not exist. Neither did Revelstoke, Banff, Calgary, Moose Jaw, Regina, or Brandon. They were

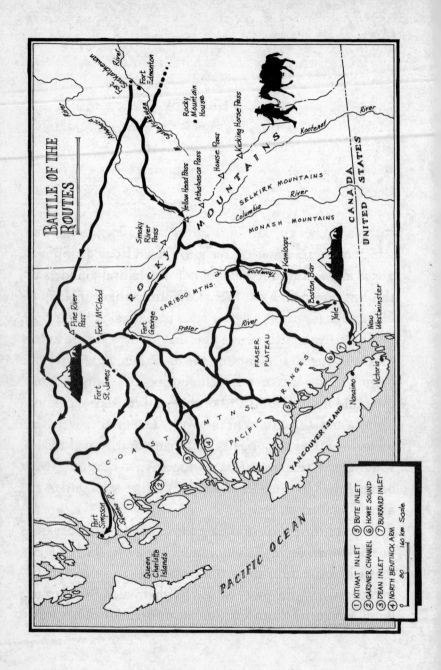

created by the railway – and so were scores of other towns and villages that sprang up when the line of steel was driven.

We built the West at the same time we built the railway, and so the saga of its construction – and a romantic and adventurous saga it is – is central to our knowledge of Canadian history. Every nation has such an epic – the *voortrek* of the Boers in what is now South Africa, the Long March of the Chinese under Mao Zedong (1934-35) , the American Civil War (1861-65), the French Revolution (1789-93), the Spanish Armada (1588). Ours is the only country in which the great epic is the building of a railway.

It's important to remember that the railway builders of the nineteenth century were operating blindly. No one knew where the western terminus would be. No one knew whether or not there were passes in the mountains through which the steel could thread its way. No one realized that there were swamps so vast that they could, and would, swallow an entire locomotive at a single gulp. No one realized the depth of the chasms in the mountains that would require the tallest wooden trestle bridges in the world.

In those days there was no mechanical earth moving equipment – no bulldozers, for instance – only horse-drawn scrapers. The railroad builders would have to tear their way through massive obstacles using the most primitive of methods.

Yet they did it, joining Canada from sea to sea and shaping a nation in the process. Today we drive from point to point along the Trans-Canada Highway that follows the railway route. We cross the Rogers Pass in the Selkirks by private car. But none of this easy sightseeing would have been possible if the railway builders hadn't done the spade work (literally in many cases) that made it all come true.

CHAPTER ONE

Walter Moberly finds a pass

IN THE SPRING OF 1871, a bearded Canadian surveyor and engineer named Walter Moberly was working in Salt Lake City, the capital of Utah, when the stunning news came that Canada had made an agreement with his native British Columbia. The pact was historic. British Columbia would join Confederation and become part of Canada if a railway could be built from central Canada to the Pacific Ocean. That line of steel would help tie the former British colony to the new nation.

The story of the building of the Canadian Pacific Railway is long and dramatic. But nothing in that story is more dramatic than the stories of the men who found the route for the line. Nobody can build a railway unless they know where it's going and how it's going to get there. Surveyors for the Pacific Railway were assigned the task of finding the easiest and best route – first across the Canadian Shield (in what is now northern Ontario), then the prairies, and finally through the mountain walls that lie between the prairies and British Columbia. Walter Moberly was one of these men.

No life was harsher than that suffered by members of the Canadian Pacific Survey crews. None was less rewarding. Underpaid and overworked, they rarely saw their families. It was not often possible for mail to reach them. They slept in slime and snow drifts, suffered from sunstroke, frostbite, scurvy, and fatigue. They often fought with one another, as happens when weary men are thrown together for long, lonely periods of isolation. And yet the surveyors kept on, year after year.

They explored great sections of Canada. The first engineers scaled mountains that had never before been climbed. They crossed lakes that had never known a white man's paddle. They forded rivers that weren't on any map. Each one walked with a uniform stride, developed through years of habit, measuring the distances as they went, checking the altitudes and examining the land with a practised gaze.

Always in their mind's eye they saw the finished line of steel – curves, grades, valley crossings, bridges and trestles, tunnels, cuts, and fills. From 1871 to 1877 they explored forty-six thousand miles (73,600 km) of Canada.

Twelve thousand of these miles (19,000 km) were then charted, foot by foot, by scores of survey parties. Axemen, following the original blazes on the trees left by the first pathfinders, hacked the lines clear of brush. Men known as chainmen – after the long surveyor's chain that measured distances – followed, dividing the line into hundred-foot (30 m) sections, each marked by a stake. Behind the chainmen came the transit men, who figured out the angle of each bend and tried to estimate those distances which a chain couldn't measure.

Behind the transits, the rodmen and levellers worked, figuring out the altitudes, and marking them every half mile (0.8 km).

And by 1877, there were twenty-five thousand of these bench marks, as they were called, and more than six hundred thousand stakes scattered across the West, from the Canadian Shield to the Pacific. By then the lives of thirty-eight men had been taken by drowning, forest fire, exposure, illness, and shipwreck.

They were a strange breed – hard-drinking, quarrelsome, jealous of each other sometimes, tough, and often strange, even weird. The members of each survey party wanted *their* route to be the one chosen for the Pacific Railway. But since the surveyors ended up discovering at least seven routes through the mountains of British Columbia, only one could be successful. Every surveyor fought to have *his* route accepted as official. That led to arguments, and sometimes fisticuffs.

Walter Moberly was sure that he knew the best – indeed the only – route through the mountains. That is why he went immediately to Ottawa, to push his case before John A. Macdonald, the prime minister.

Every surveyor tends to fall in love with the new country he explores. Moberly had fallen in love with a notch in the Gold Range (now the Monashee Mountains). This was

Eagle Pass, which he had discovered and named back in the summer of 1865 after watching a flight of eagles winging their way through the mountains.

Moberly knew that eagles generally follow a stream, or make for an opening in the wall of granite. And so he followed the route of the birds and discovered the pass he was seeking.

For many years Moberly would tell the romantic story of how he finally left his companions after a sleepless night and made his way down into the valley of the Eagle River. There he hacked out a blaze on a tree, and wrote the announcement: "This is the Pass for the Overland Railway." And, as it turned out many years later, he was right.

Now, in the fall of 1871, with a pact made with British Columbia and survey gangs being assembled, Moberly high-tailed it for Ottawa. His rival, Alfred Waddington, was already trying to start a railway company, and Moberly hated Waddington. In fact, he hated anyone who tried to promote any railway route to the Pacific other than the one he had discovered through Eagle Pass.

Waddington was a fanatic on the subject of the Pacific coast's Bute Inlet as an end-point for the railway. He had explored it. But Moberly was just as fanatical on the subject of Eagle Pass. In Moberly's view, the railway should run through Eagle Pass and down the Fraser River into Burrard Inlet, the present site of Vancouver – south of Bute Inlet. He considered Burrard *his* inlet. He had trudged along its shores before any white man settled there. Now he meant to present his case to the prime minister himself.

Walter Moberly had gone to school in Barrie with a tawny-haired girl named Suzanne Agnes Bernard. Now she was Lady Macdonald, wife of the prime minister. And of course, when Moberly turned up in Ottawa, that spring of 1871, she invited her former schoolmate to lunch at Earnscliffe, the prime minister's turreted residence on the Ottawa River.

Here, the weather-beaten surveyor, with his long ragged beard and burning eyes, pressed his vision of the railway on Macdonald. With supreme confidence he insisted he could tell the prime minister exactly where to locate the line from the prairies to the seacoast. He went even farther. "You can commence construction of the line six weeks after I get back to British Columbia," he said firmly.

That, as things turned out, was more than impossible. But surveyors were not only a hardy breed, they were also an optimistic breed. And Moberly had to add a postscript to what he said. "Of course, I don't know how many millions you have," he announced, "but it's going to cost you money to get through those canyons." The prime minister was impressed.

Moberly was a fighter who came from a family of fighters. He was half Polish – his mother's father had been in command of the Russian artillery at the famous Battle of Borodino, which effectively stopped Napoleon, the French emperor, in his march towards Moscow.

Moberly's father was a captain in the Royal Navy. As a young engineer, Moberly had worked on the Northern Railway between Toronto and Collingwood, excited by

Walter Moberly crashes through the ice of British Columbia's Shuswap Lake.

tales of the frontier. The Fraser gold rush of 1848 took him west. And there, in 1859, he helped lay out the city of New Westminster near the Burrard Inlet.

It was Moberly who had also located, surveyed, and built part of the historic corduroy road from Yale on the Fraser River north to the Cariboo goldfields, over which thousands of would-be prospectors trudged, or rattled in carriages, or rode on horseback to reach the fabled treasure.

But he was a better surveyor than businessman. The road left him in debt. It took him eight years to pay off what he owed. And like so many surveyors of that time he was also in politics. But he resigned his seat in the legislature to take the post of assistant surveyor general for British Columbia. It was in that role that he discovered the Eagle Pass in the Gold Range.

Now he was returning to British Columbia with the prime minister's blessing. He would be district engineer in charge of the region between Shuswap Lake, to the west of the Gold Range, and the eastern foothills of the Rockies. Moberly was about to turn forty. He was as flexible as a willow and as tough as tempered steel. He was probably the best axeman in the country – and every surveyor had to be an axeman to fight his way through the jungles of the British Columbia rain forest.

Moberly never seemed to tire. He had a passion for dancing and, when he emerged from the wilderness, he would dance the night out in Victoria. He loved to drink, and he loved to sing, but as one friend said, "No amount of relaxation and conviviality would impair his staying power when he plunged into the wilds again."

He had as many lives as a cat. Once, while on horseback in the Athabaska country, he was swept into a river and carried two hundred feet (60 m) downstream. He seized an overhanging tree, hauled himself from the saddle, and climbed to safety.

On a cold January day he fell through the ice of Shuswap Lake and very nearly drowned, for the surface was so rotten it broke under his hands. Almost exhausted from his struggle in the icy water, he managed somehow to pull the snowshoes from his feet and, with one in each hand, he spread out his arms on the ice and climbed to safety.

Another time on the Columbia River he gave chase in a spruce bark canoe to a bear. He cornered the animal against the riverbank, put an old military pistol against its ear and shot it dead, seizing it by its hind legs before it sank – all at very great risk, not to mention the terror and the fear of his companions in the frail craft.

He was, in short, a "character." He was vain, stubborn, and very independent. He wouldn't work with anybody he didn't agree with. That was a problem, because Moberly disagreed with anyone who thought there was any railway route to the Pacific other than the one that he had in his mind. He'd been thinking about the railway longer than most of his colleagues – ever since his explorations in 1858. And now thirteen years later he set out to confirm his findings.

He began on July 20, 1871, the very day the new province entered Confederation. His favourite mountain area was bounded by the Eagle Pass of the Gold Range and the Howse Pass in the Rockies, just north of the now famous Kicking Horse. This was the area in which he was to take charge.

Between these two mountain chains, the Gold Range to the west and the Rockies to the east, lay an island of frightening peaks – the apparently unclimbable Selkirks. It was in the hairpin-shaped trench around this barrier that the Columbia River flowed, first northwest, then southeast again, until it passed within a few miles of its source. Moberly believed that the railway should cut through the Rockies by the Howse Pass. It would then coil around the Selkirks by following the Columbia valley. After that it would make its way through the Gold Range by "his" Eagle Pass. That would lead to Kamloops, and the canyons of the Fraser.

He spent the next eight months in the mountains and trenches of British Columbia. He travelled down the olive-green Columbia, with a crazy flotilla of leaky boats, burned-out logs, and bark canoes, patched with old rags and bacon grease.

He trudged up and down the sides of mountains, hanging on to the reins of his pack horses, always with a faithful company of Indians, for whom he showed greater respect than he did for the white man. He said that the Indian, "when properly handled and made to feel that confidence and trust is reposed in him, will work in all kinds of weather, and should supplies run short, on little or no food, without a murmur; not so the generality of white men."

Like so many of his colleagues, who were forced to fend for themselves in the wilderness and survive, he was a difficult and prickly man. He was also a very good surveyor, which makes his personal tragedy all the more bitter. For, as we shall see, Walter Moberly, the man who first found a pass for the railway, was doomed to disappointment.

Chapter Two

Life on a survey gang

To understand a surveyor's life, it is fascinating to examine the story of one ordinary surveyor. For Moberly, certainly, life could be disappointing, but it was also stimulating. But for the men under him, the axemen, the packers, the chainmen, the levellers, the rodmen – it could be pitiless. Fortunately we have the record of one such man who left a diary behind him. His name was Robert M. Rylatt. He was a former sergeant with the Royal Engineers. Moberly hired him to take charge of the pack train of supplies for Party "S" to survey the Howse Pass in the Rockies that summer of 1871.

Rylatt had a distinguished career as a soldier. He won three medals fighting the Turkish Army on the Danube in Eastern Europe and later in the Crimean War (1853-56). He came to Canada as part of an engineering party under Colonel R. C. Moody, the man who laid out New Westminster, the first capital of the new colony of British Columbia. But for all of his few years in Canada, he was facing tragedy. His wife had become a hopeless invalid, and

Rylatt desperately needed money. And so, with some misgivings, he signed on with Walter Moberly for the ordeal of his life.

The job would take him away from his wife for almost two years. His description of that "painful hour of parting" is heart-rending. Rising from her pillow, his wife Jane cried out "Oh, Bob, I shall never see you again."

Rylatt hastened off, "fearing each step to hear her cries." On the steamboat that took him away, he wrote, "I felt as if I had ruthlessly abandoned her, as every stroke of the paddles bore me further from her."

But that was the life of a surveyor in days of the Canadian Pacific Survey. Long periods of isolation and long periods of hunger were their lot. But had Rylatt known what lay ahead he would never have signed a contract with the Canadian Pacific Railway.

Once he began there was no way he could quit. He was actually a prisoner in the mountains, walled off by a five-hundred-mile (800 km) barrier of granite peaks and impassable forests, which few men would dare to penetrate by themselves. He thought the job would take a year. He left New Westminster in July of 1871. He didn't get back until June of 1873.

So here he was, a member of Survey Party "S". His immediate boss was E.C. Gillette, an American engineer with a good reputation whom Moberly had known for years. Under Gillette were four surveyors and sixteen men – mainly axemen hired to chop their way through the difficult forests – together with eight Mexican and Indian packers, who carried the biggest loads, and one man, a hunter, who brought in fresh meat. The forty-five pack animals also carried close to seven tons (6.4 tonnes) of food and equipment.

In order to reach the Rocky Mountains, this cumbersome party, loaded down with goods and supplies, had to struggle over hills littered with loose boulders, and make their way through mud holes so deep that the horses were mired to their bellies.

Rylatt was in charge of the pack train. And so, over and over again, he had to go through the tiring business of unloading each horse, hauling him out of the mud, and reloading him again. Some couldn't be saved. As he wrote:

"How worried would be any member of the Humane society, could he see the treatment animals in a Pack Train receive, where the animals themselves are only a secondary consideration, the open sores on their backs, from hard and incessant packing, angry and running with humour, over which the Packer, too often, if not closely watched, without waiting throws the heavy *apparajos* or Pack saddle, and as the cinch [*he spells it 'sinch*] is tightened ... the poor beast groans, rears and plunges and not unfrequently sinks down under the pain, only to be whipped again into position."

The axemen moved ahead of the horses. It was their job to hack their way through the massive network of fallen cedars and to cut tunnels in a green tangle as thick as any Borneo jungle. After that they laid down patches of corduroy – literally a wooden roadway made of logs – for the animals to cross.

The men pushed straight across the Selkirk Mountains into the Kootenay country. They didn't reach the upper Columbia until late September. They headed down this roaring river on rafts and in small canoes, watching with growing alarm as it swelled in size with every mile. On the third day, the raft on which Rylatt was travelling hit a submerged log in the rapids and was sucked under. The five

Robert Rylatt and his crew hit a log in the rapids.

men on the raft leaped for the shore. One fell short, the current pulled him under with the raft, and he was never seen again.

At the mouth of the Blaeberry River, which flows down from the summit of Howse Pass to join the Columbia, the axemen were faced with a daunting task. It was their job to chop a pathway to the top, through forests that had not been trodden since the pass had been discovered a dozen years before. The autumn winds had reduced the country

to a muck so thick that one mule couldn't be pulled out of it. Rylatt was forced to shoot him in his swampy prison.

And yet there were moments of great beauty and mystery. And here among the silent peaks Rylatt was moved. On his first Sunday in the mountains he found himself alone – the others were working five miles (8 km) farther up the pass. This was his first experience in the wilderness and he made the most of it.

He watched the sun drop down behind the glaciers on the mountaintops. The day's dying light tipped the snows with a gold that turned to red, while in the shadowed gorges the ice could be seen in long streaks of filmy blue. Rylatt watched as the glow left the peaks and the gloom filled up the valleys. He continued to watch as velvet night followed ghostly twilight. And he saw the pale rays of the northern lights compete with the stars to cast softening halos of light on those everlasting snowfields.

Then suddenly he began to shiver. A sense of terrible loneliness overcame him. It was the silence – the uncanny overpowering silence of the Canadian wilderness. Not a leaf stirred, no insect hummed, not even the noise of the water in the creek far away broke the silence. Rylatt listened for a sound, but he didn't hear even the rustle of a falling leaf. He made a fire. It wasn't that he wanted just to keep warm, he wanted to hear *something* – the crackling of the wood – to break the loneliness. It occurred to him that no one who had not experienced what he was going through would ever understand what it was like to be truly alone.

He wrote in his diary: "Your sense of being alone in the heart of the city, or even in a village, or within easy distance of fellow beings … gives you no claim to use the term 'alone'. You may have the feeling peculiar to being alone – that is all. Listen sometime when you think you are alone…. can you hear a footfall; a door slam in the distance; a carriage go by? Or the rumble of one … ? Can you hear a dog bark? Have you a cricket on the hearth or even the ticking of a clock … ?"

Now he realized for the first time that the tiniest of sounds could give a feeling of relief – "the sense of knowing your species are at no great distance." But here, in the solitude of the Rockies, there was only the terrible silence.

His sense of isolation was increased by the onset of winter. The mail did not come. Now Gillette and his men began chopping their pathway to the top of the pass. By the time the trail was opened on October 26, the snow was already falling.

The next day, with eight inches (20 cm) blanketing the mountains, Walter Moberly and the surveyors gathered at the summit of the Howse Pass, ready at last to start work. But the instruments were so full of water they were useless, while the slopes were so slippery with wet snow that no man could maintain a footing.

The next day another foot (30 cm) of snow fell. Now the engineers realized that nothing more could be done. The party settled down for a long winter at the foot of the pass about one hundred miles (160 km) north of the present site of Banff. It would be May before the mountain trails would be passable again. For those sections that ran through the canyons it would be much later.

It wouldn't really be safe to travel with loaded pack horses before June. Even then the mountain torrents could be crossed only with difficulty, being swollen with melting snow from above. And so the twenty-nine members of the party, including (as it turned out) two ex-convicts, were faced with each other's company for six or seven months.

Every man in that party worried about getting his mail and getting his wages. Because of bungling it would be months before they saw a pay cheque. A civil servant in Victoria – a political appointee – had kept the money, banked it, and taken the interest for himself. And the mail wasn't forwarded. It lay around for months in various post offices, because no plans had been made to handle it. To get it one of the packers set off in late November for Wild Horse Creek, a five-hundred-mile (800 km) journey on snowshoes.

He brought some letters back, but none for Rylatt, who was sick with worry over his wife's condition. That night he scribbled in his diary, "Poor wife, are you dead or alive? Have the two deposits of money I sent reached you? It may easily be understood in my case, how hard it is to receive no word, no sign, and altogether I am very miserable."

The only link with civilization was Walter Moberly himself. He left camp on December 4, heading for New Westminster. En route he planned to trek across the high barrier of the Selkirk Mountains, hoping to find a pass for the railway somewhere in that wilderness of jagged peaks. He took one man with him, a Frenchman named Verdier who had just learned that his wife had eloped, leaving their five children alone. Rylatt sent a note with some money to his own wife with Verdier, knowing there would be no further word from her until the following May or June.

New Westminster, the nearest pin-point of civilization, was four hundred miles (640 km) away, but Moberly travelled it as casually as if he were setting off on a pleasant Sunday hike. He went straight over the tops of the glaciers that cover the Selkirks, hoping to find a gap in that mountain wall through which the railway might go. On New Year's Day, 1872, he was all alone in an abandoned trapper's hut. He wrote in his diary, "I think it … one of the most wretched and dreary places I ever saw … this was the most wretched New Year's Day I ever spent."

In spite of his long trek across the Selkirk Mountains, Walter Moberly did not find what he was seeking. When he reached Victoria he reported to his boss, Sandford Fleming in Ottawa, that there was no practical pass through that long rampart of chiselled peaks. He would have to find some other way of getting the railway through British Columbia to the coast.

CHAPTER THREE

~

"The Jolly C.P.S."

BY 1872, SANDFORD FLEMING, Moberly's boss, had dispatched twenty-one survey parties – a total of eight hundred men – across the country to lay out the route of the Pacific Railway.

The engineer-in-chief was a huge man with a vast beard and an awesome reputation. At the age of forty-five he still had half his life ahead of him in which to complete the Intercolonial Railway in the Maritimes, plan the Canadian Pacific, devise a workable system of Standard Time, promote the Pacific cable, act as ambassador to Hawaii, publish a book of short prayers, become chancellor of Queen's University in Kingston, Ont., girdle the globe and cross Canada by foot, snowshoe, dog team, horseback, dugout canoe, and, finally, by rail.

He was a dedicated amateur, whose interests ranged from a study of early steamboats to colour blindness. He was a competent artist, a better than average chess player, an amateur lawyer, a graceful public speaker, a prolific diarist and author who, at his death, had some 150 articles, reports, books, and pamphlets to his credit. It was Fleming who, back in 1862, had come up with the first credible plan for a Pacific railway. Now it was his task to put that plan into practice.

It would not be easy.

A very special kind of man was needed, and, as Fleming reported after his first season, it was impossible to find enough of them.

"Many of those we were obliged to take," he wrote, "were unequal to the very arduous labour they had to undergo," causing a very considerable delay and difficulty in pushing the work.

Fleming was soon reporting that it was impossible to hire the kind of men he needed for the survey. In 1871, for example, two crews in northern Ontario simply gave up the ghost. One party had had enough by the late summer; the second, learning they would be required to stay out all winter, "suffered a few days of cold and snow, and then promptly trooped into Fort Garry" near present-day Winnipeg. There weren't enough good men to do the job and Fleming and his staff had to employ incompetents.

The wonder was that anyone worked on the surveys at all. In spite of the difficulty of getting men each year, there was little job security – even for the most experienced engineers. Crews were dropped at the end of the summer, and left without any winter work, and not rehired again until the following spring.

They led a lonely, remote existence – cut off from news

of family, friends, or the world at large, in a land where the native rites and customs were as foreign as those of an Oriental kingdom. One surveyor, Henry Cambie (a street in Vancouver is now named for him), found that out. Exploring the east branch of the Homathco River in central British Columbia, Cambie came upon a band of Indians who were so far away from civilization that many of the women had never seen a beard "and would not believe that mine really grew on my chin."

Another surveyor named Jason Allard, who worked for Moberly, made the mistake of accepting an invitation to visit an Indian lodge. He made the second mistake of sitting on a bear rug next to a good-looking Indian woman. He realized too late that this was the same as an offer of marriage. The only way he could get out of it was to trade her back to her father for a handsome finger ring.

And yet they went out, year after year – men who for the most part were tough, intelligent, and uncomplaining. They drank heavily. And when they drank they sang their theme song – the song of the Canadian Pacific Survey:

> Far away from those we love dearest,
>   Who long and wish for home,
> The thought of whom each lone heart cheereth,
>   As 'mid these North-west wilds we roam,
> Yet still each one performs his duty
>   And gaily sings:
> Tra, la, la, la, la, la, la, la, la, la, la,

Hurra! The jolly C.P.S.!
They're at home upon Superior's shore,
Hurra! we'll drink to them success,
And a safe return once more.

But it was often a nightmare just to reach that "home upon Superior's shore." Charles Aeneas Shaw, who was with the survey for the whole of its existence, remembered his own initiation in November of 1872. Shaw, then eighteen years old, was hired as a packer by a party trying to locate a line west from Prince Arthur's Landing (now Thunder Bay, Ont.).

The trick was to try to reach the landing before winter sealed off the lake. The survey party tried first in a tiny little steamer, the *Mary Ward*. The boat hit a reef in a howling blizzard, and three of the men drowned. The rest returned to Toronto and picked up new kits and then set off again.

They made their way overland to Duluth in the United States. There they offered to pay as much as $2,500 for a tugboat to take them up the lake. But conditions were so desperate no seasoned skipper would attempt the crossing. However, the party bought a small fishing boat and in mid-December started rowing and sailing to their destination.

Imagine the situation! The temperature sank to 52 degrees below zero (-47° C) – so cold that each crewman had to chip from the blades of his oars a ball of ice the size of a man's head. They crept along the shoreline, sleeping in the snow at night, living on frozen pork and hardtack, and even

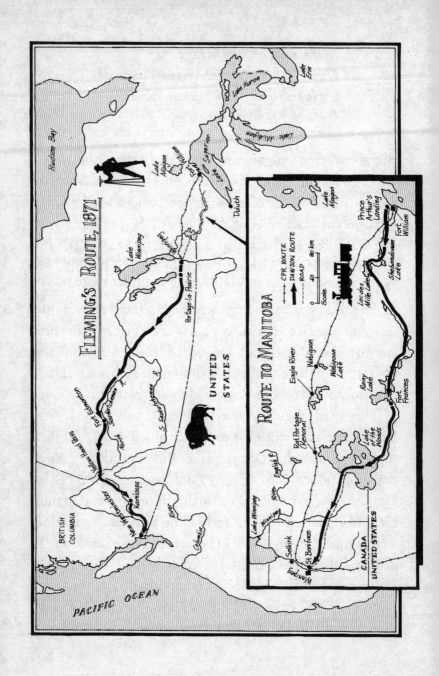

FLEMING'S ROUTE, 1871

ROUTE TO MANITOBA

surviving a full-force gale. On New Year's Day the lake froze and they abandoned the boat. They built toboggans out of strips sawn from frozen birch logs, and then hiked with their supplies the last fifty miles to Prince Arthur's Landing.

Such hardships were commonplace. One man, J.H.E. Secretan, was reduced to eating rose haws washed down with swamp water during a survey near Lake Nipigon in 1871. That same year – the year in which Robert Rylatt was toiling in the Rockies – seven members of a survey supply party were lost near Jackfish River in northern Ontario, as a result of a forest fire so hot the very soil was burned away. Only one body was found. Of the remainder there was no trace, except for six holes scratched out in a nearby swamp and apparently left behind when the smoke grew too thick.

It was difficult to get supplies to these isolated men, and that resulted in costly delays and bitter arguments. Henry Carre, in charge of a party working out of Lac des Isles in the Thunder Bay area, found himself in a country through which no white man had ever travelled. He couldn't finish his survey because his supplies couldn't reach him, and he had to turn back. Otherwise, he said, "I verily believe the whole party would have been starved to death."

Another surveyor, working near Long Lake north of Superior that same year, had to take his party off surveying to pick blueberries to save their lives. The group had had nothing to eat for a week.

One survey party, working north of Wabigoon west of Prince Arthur's Landing, were caught by the winter

Surveyor Edward Jarvis and company find their way blocked by a box canyon.

without toboggans, tents, clothing or boots. Their leader, William Kirkpatrick, a resourceful man, made forty pairs of snowshoes and thirty toboggans with his own hands. Then he sewed up a tent out of canvas and borrowed another made of skins from the Indians so his people wouldn't freeze to death.

In the winter of 1871 in the Thompson River country of central B.C., forty miles (64 km) out of Kamloops, one survey party lost almost all of its pack animals. Eighty-six died from cold, hunger, or overwork.

There was an even worse work expedition in 1875. The leader of that party, E.W. Jarvis, was given the job of examining the Smoky River Pass in the northern Rockies. He set off in January with two companions, six Indians, and twenty dogs.

The stories he and his comrades have left behind present an uncanny series of spectacles – almost like a sequence in a modern motion picture:

– the eerie figure of Alec McDonald in charge of the dog trains, knocking on the door of the shack in 49 below zero (-45° C) weather, sheathed in ice from head to toe.

– the spectacle of the lead dog who made a feeble effort to rise, gave one final flick of his tail, and rolled over dead. His legs were frozen stiff to the shoulders.

– the weird noises heard one night by the entire party – the distinct but ghostly sound of a tree being felled two hundred yards (183 m) away, without any signs of snowshoes or axemanship to be seen the following morning.

The Jarvis party travelled light, with two blankets for each man and a single piece of light cotton sheeting for a tent. They moved through a land that had never been explored. A good deal of the time they had no idea where they were.

They camped out in temperatures that had dropped to 53 below (-47° C). They fell through thin ice and had to climb out soaked to the skin, with their snowshoes still tied to their feet. They stumbled down deep canyons and found the way blocked by frozen waterfalls two hundred feet (61 m) high.

One day they experienced a sudden change of temperature. It went from 42 below (-41° C) to 40 above (4° C). This brought on a strange weariness – as if they were suddenly plunged into the tropics.

One morning, while mushing down a frozen river, they turned a corner and saw an abyss yawning before them. The entire party was perched on an ice ledge of a frozen waterfall 210 feet (64 m) high. And the ledge itself was no more than two feet (0.6 m) thick!

One night they camped below a blue glacier when, without warning, great chunks of it gave way. Above them they could see masses of ice and rock chasing one another and leaping from point to point "as if playing some weird, gigantic game." One chunk of limestone, ten feet (3 m) thick, scudded past them, tearing a tunnel through the trees before it plunged into the river.

By March the dogs were dying. Even the Indians were in a mournful state of despair, declaring they would never see their homes again and weeping bitterly. Jarvis was very thin and very white and very quiet. They had reached the Smoky Pass but Jarvis was doubtful about going farther. His assistant, C.F. Hannington, said however that he would rather starve than turn back. And now it began to look as if he would:

"I have been thinking of 'the dearest spot on earth to me,'" Hannington wrote in his journal, " – of our Mother and Father and all my brothers and sisters and friends – of the happy days at home – of all the good deeds I have left undone and all the bad ones committed. If ever our bones will be discovered, when and by whom. If our friends will mourn long for us or do as is often done, forget us as soon as possible. In short, I have been looking death in the face…."

Meanwhile Jarvis felt a curious kind of numbness taking hold of his limbs. They pushed forward on their snowshoes looking like men marking time in slow motion. And yet they made it.

Hannington had lost thirty-three pounds (15 kg), Jarvis was down to a bony 125 (57 kg). When they were finally given food in Edmonton, in what is now Alberta, they fell sick and began to vomit, but still they kept on across the blizzard-swept prairies until they reached Fort Garry. They had spent 116 days on the trail, and had travelled 1,887 miles (3,019 km). Nine hundred and thirty-two of those miles (1,491 km) were covered on snowshoes. When the dogs died they carried on with all of their goods on their backs.

Why did they do it? Why did any of them do it? They

certainly didn't do it for profit. There was little enough of that. Nor did they do it for adventure – there was too much of that.

The answer seems clear from what they wrote and what they did. Each man did it for glory. Each man was driven by the slender, but always present hope, that someday his name would be recognized and placed on the map, on a mountain peak, or a river, or an inlet, or – glory of glories – would go into the history books as the one who had bested all others and located the route for the great railway.

CHAPTER FOUR

~

Moberly disobeys orders

EVEN THOUGH WALTER MOBERLY hadn't found a way through the high Selkirk Mountains he was convinced that he had found the right pass through the Rockies. The Howse Pass was *his* pass; he had found it, he had surveyed it, he owned it. He was absolutely sure that this was the only route the railway could take. After that it would have to get around the Selkirks by following the big bend of the Columbia River, and then work its way through the Gold Range by the Eagle Pass, which he had also discovered.

In spite of the fact that Sandford Fleming had twenty-one teams of surveyors out searching for different routes, Walter Moberly was convinced that his route was the only one that would work. He was so sure of himself that without anybody's permission he started to locate an actual line for the railway through the Howse Pass.

Moberly figured he would get the permission later and that Fleming, his boss, would back him. But all that Fleming wanted and agreed to was known as a simple "trial line" through the pass. That simply meant a series of blazes on trees to find out if it were at all practical for a railway.

Moberly was planning something far more ambitious – and without permission! He wanted a detailed *location* survey. That is the kind that engineers make only when finally, through exploration and trial lines, they have firmly decided on the route.

Moberly hadn't done that. He'd walked through the pass, but made only a brief investigation of a route from the summit to the Columbia River. All the same, that spring of 1872, he set about hiring extra men, taking on trains of pack animals, and buying thousands of dollars' worth of supplies, great quantities of which he planned to cache at Eagle Pass. He figured it would take two seasons to locate the line. He and his men were prepared to stay out all winter.

And then just four hours before he and his party were scheduled to leave Victoria, the British Columbia capital on Vancouver Island, for the interior, he received a staggering blow. A telegram arrived, literally at the eleventh hour, since the boat was scheduled to leave at three in the morning. It was from Fleming announcing that another pass had officially been adopted for the route of the Canadian Pacific Railway.

Fleming's pass, far to the north, was the Yellow Head Pass two hundred miles (320 km) west of present-day Edmonton. The chief surveyor ordered Moberly to abandon the Howse Pass and to move his survey parties north. He would go by way of the Athabaska Pass, and then take a charge of a survey through the Yellow Head. All Moberly's dreams dissolved at that moment. "His" route was not to be *the* route, after all.

He rushed to Portland, Oregon, where he had to buy his way out of the costly contracts he'd signed. Unfortunately most of the supplies that he ordered had been already dispatched to the remote mountain areas where they could never be used. Seven thousand dollars' worth were abandoned forever at the Eagle Pass.

Another problem raised its head. Moberly would need to hire pack trains to move men and supplies from the original position, north to the Athabaska country where Fleming wanted him. But it was late in the season. Most pack trains were engaged far in advance, when it was cheap to rent pack animals. Moberly realized that if the packers knew his problem, they would hike up the prices. So he'd have to get around the packers who were heading for the Howse Pass, race on ahead of them, intercept them, and then reorder the horses for the Yellow Head survey before the owners caught on to the change of plans.

Off he went. First he headed through Oregon by stagecoach, which broke down. And then by steamboat, which sank. He continued on through the state of Washington on horseback, and re-entered British Columbia in the Kootenay country. There he successfully intercepted the packers and hired them all, together with four hundred horses. Hacking a trail through the jungle-like growth as he went, he finally reached the Columbia River.

On May 15, he reached his party at the Howse Pass, told

them the route had been abandoned and the party must move north to the Athabaska country, and to the despised Yellow Head Pass. Fleming, who was travelling across Canada along the proposed future line of the railway, had agreed to meet him there. But it was heavy going for Moberly. The pack trail had literally to be carved, foot by foot, out of the tangle of falling cedars that barred the way up through the cavernous valleys of the Columbia, the Thompson, and the Albreda Rivers.

He finally reached the Yellow Head in early September. One day, just west of Jasper House, he came upon fresh tracks, which the Indians told him were those of "men of the East." A short time later he ran into the Reverend Doctor James Grant, who was the principal of Queen's University and Fleming's companion on his trans-Canada trek. Grant carried a long stick in his hand and was "driving some worn-out and very dilapidated pack animals."

The meeting that followed must have been disagreeable to both Moberly and Fleming. Grant didn't mention it in his book about the trip. He simply wrote that Moberly's was the first face they had seen since leaving the prairies. To meet him, Grant said, was "like reopening communication with the world....how welcome he was, we need not say!" Fleming thought differently.

That evening everybody had a glass of punch and cigar on Fleming. They drank toasts to the Queen and to the country. Moberly put Grant in a good humour because he had some oatmeal, and so the minister could finally enjoy a

Sunday breakfast of porridge for the first time in many days. Fleming decided to wait until the Sunday service was over before confronting Moberly. The twenty-one men from both sides of the mountains – English, Scots, Irish, and Indians – representing every one of the six Canadian provinces, joined in the hymn singing. Grant preached a sermon. Then, finally, Moberly made his report to his chief.

This must have been a painful interview. Fleming was aghast at the slow progress made, and even more by Moberly's reckless spending on useless supplies, tons of which had been left forever at Eagle Pass. "It seemed to me as if some country store had been bought out when I first saw the account," he later recalled. Imagine: four hundred pack horses! Why so many? The engineer couldn't understand it. He decided to fire Moberly but then realized he couldn't afford to do that. Somebody had to take charge at the Yellow Head and push the surveys forward. Moberly was the only one with enough experience.

Moberly was disgusted with Fleming and not about to take a verbal spanking from him. In abandoning his pet line, he thought Fleming had been positively "unpatriotic." To use any other pass than his, was, in his own mind, little short of treason.

He was prepared to leave the service, but he couldn't because of the men and animals he had left to winter at the Howse Pass. He knew that they relied on him to see them safely through. After Fleming and his party had left, Moberly began to worry over the slow progress of the survey under his command. Bad luck seemed to dog his footsteps. The parties were taking a long time to arrive. In fact, with Moberly out of the way, they had simply sat down to wait out the winter.

Chapter Five

The ordeal of Robert Rylatt

BY THE END OF 1871 Robert Rylatt had come to the end of his tether. He felt he had reached the very bottom. Moberly had gone on his wild goose chase across the Selkirks. Then one day Rylatt cut his thumb and opened a small roll of bandage material his wife had stowed in his kit. It brought back sad memories.

"When I saw scraps of oiled silk, fingers of old gloves, and the softest of lint, how tenderly I felt towards her, but when a slip of paper came to light, on which were the words 'God bless you, Bob' it made me feel wretched...."

On Christmas Day the thermometer dropped to 34 below zero (-37° C). The following day the mercury froze solid. Although Christmas dinner was served piping hot, the food was frozen to the plates before the men could consume it.

By New Year's Eve 1871 – the same evening that saw Moberly alone in a cabin in the Selkirks – Rylatt felt he had reached rock bottom. He and four others sat in their cabin seeing the old year out, trying to keep warm. Though a

Robert Rylatt holds off a mutiny at the cookhouse door:

rousing fire had been lit, each man had to change position constantly so that the side of his body away from the heat did not become numbed with cold.

They talked of their wives and other adventures they had had; but there was no mirth. When they looked at their watches and saw that it was the New Year, they crept into their blankets. It was quite a time before Rylatt slept, for his brain was haunted by past memories. It was the first time he had not spent the New Year with his wife.

Four more months of this prison-like existence lay ahead. Personal angers had been bubbling beneath the surface, and now began to burst out. Rylatt and the chief surveyor, Gillette, had been speaking to each other only when necessary. In one argument Gillette had thrown a grouse bone in Rylatt's face. Rylatt had replied with a cup of hot coffee. At that point Gillette had threatened to shoot him.

By February Rylatt had a deadly hatred for his boss. He was convinced Gillette was going crazy. Gillette felt the same way about Rylatt.

Rylatt wrote in his diary: "That man, Gillette, is not only a fool but an unmanly cur, deserving the sympathy of none, and the power that pitched forth such a being into even our rough society, and placed him pro tem at the head of it, ought to be blackballed." Gillette threatened to drill a hole in Rylatt with his pistol.

The absolute lack of activity soured the tempers of the party. Rylatt, in March, noted in his diary: "The roughs of the party are in open mutiny. Growling at their food, cursing me for being out of sugar; all this I care little for … but my pent up feelings found vent today, and the leader of the roughs will carry my mark to his grave. I have been through somewhat an exciting scene and don't care to have it repeated."

This is what had happened: seven of the most mutinous members of the party had gathered at the cookhouse door, planning to rush it and seize the food and sugar they wrongly believed Rylatt was secretly hoarding.

In the argument that followed, Rylatt was threatened by the ringleader, an Australian ex-convict named Roberts. Then Rylatt snatched up a hatchet, and when Roberts made a move towards him, he chopped off three of his fingers.

That drove off the mob, but they came back in an hour armed with axes. Rylatt held them off with his rifle, and stayed on guard until they quieted down.

As the sun grew warmer in April, and the river ice showed signs of breaking up, much of this ill humour disappeared. At last, in May, some mail arrived. But still Rylatt had no word of his wife. The man who had agreed to carry letters from Wild Horse Creek to Hope on the Fraser the previous fall had perished in the snows. His body was not discovered until the spring. The mail bag lay beside it.

Rylatt was frantic with anxiety. "I cannot understand why no line has reached me from my wife," he wrote. "Is she dead? … the suspense is terrible … surely someone of our many acquaintants would have let me know.…

Generally people are ready to signal bad news. My chum Jack had bad news; his house being burned down. His wife it would appear was enjoying herself at a Ball…. he lost everything…."

On May 6 Rylatt had got it into his head that his wife wasn't dead but had gone out of her mind, and this thought haunted him.

And then on May 15 Walter Moberly arrived with the startling news that the Howse Pass route had been abandoned. All their work had been useless. Moberly ordered the party to quit its headquarters on the Columbia, and move north. He knew it would be touch and go. The high Athabaska Pass was many miles away, and they would have to get to it before the blizzards blocked it and cut them off from the work at the Yellow Head.

But Rylatt had some good news at last. Moberly had a letter from Rylatt's wife. He had been carrying it around so long, the cover had been worn away. Rylatt got it on May 15, 1872. It was dated October 9, 1871.

Moberly dealt swiftly with the mutineers and with Gillette, whom he blamed for the troubles. Four of the malcontents were dismissed. Gillette was suspended. A new man, Ashdowne Green, was put in charge of the party.

As Rylatt wrote, "I cannot forget the look of hatred on Roberts's face as, upon my leaving in the boat, he held up to my sight his mutilated hand and exclaimed: 'You see this; it will help me to remember you!'"

Gillette tried to carry out his threat to shoot Rylatt. But

A huge grizzly bear attacks Kinbasket, chief of the Kootenays.

as his hand reached for the pistol in his belt, Rylatt knocked him down with a heavy blow, and another member of the party restrained his arms.

Guided by Chief Kinbasket of the Kootenay Indians, "a daring little shrivelled up old fellow," the party started on the long journey north. They were forced to break a trail for their pack horses as they moved through dense clouds of mosquitoes. Rylatt had smothered his face with mosquito muslin, and smeared his hands with bacon grease. But nothing kept them off. The heat only melted the grease and sent it under his clothing.

Then, in mid-August, a grizzly bear attacked Chief Kinbasket, who barely had time to raise his axe and aim a blow before the weapon was dashed aside. In a moment he was in the embrace of the monster. The huge forepaws gripped and the immense claws tore into his back. The bear held the Indian up and fastening the chief's shoulder in his jaws raised one of his hind feet, tore a gash, commencing at the abdomen and cutting through to the bowels – fairly stripping the flesh and muscles from one of his sides.

They didn't find Chief Kinbasket until the following morning. Miraculously he was still alive and, more miraculously, he survived. But the party had lost its trailblazer.

In late September they reached the boat encampment at the big bend of the Columbia River. Now the route took a right angle towards the Rockies and the foot of the Athabaska Pass. But it seemed impossible to reach the Yellow Head before the winter set in.

The party hesitated. And there, in the shadow of the glowering peaks, with the brooding forests hanging over them, and the moon glistening on the great rustling river, they indulged in a weird caper. On September 22 they held a grand ball.

"Think of it," Rylatt wrote in his diary, "a dance – and an enjoyable dance at that."

The best whistler in the party became "the orchestra." He knew all the latest dance tunes – "Little Brown Jug," "The Man on the Flying Trapeze," "Shoe-Fly Don't Bother Me." As Rylatt wrote, "He puckered his mouth, beat loud time on an empty soap box with a stick, and the graceful forms began to whirl." The dancers were deadly serious. Several were assigned the role of a lady partner, and later allowed to change about.

Rylatt described his assistant, Dick White, dancing with one such "lady," a great six-footer, hairy-faced, and with a fist like a sledge, pants tucked into boots still covered with river mud, "while Dick, with eyeglasses adjusted, held the huge hand gingerly by the tips of his fingers, then circling the waist of this delicate creature with the gentleness due to modesty and the fair sex, his lovely partner occasionally letting out a yell of hilarity would roll the quid of tobacco to his other cheek of his sweet face, discharging the juice beneath the feet of the dancers."

The dancing grew wilder as the full moon shed its light on the scene. When the whistler gave out, the dancers themselves shouted the tunes aloud. The entire crew seemed to have forgotten where they were. In their minds they saw themselves in some vast ballroom far from the dripping forests, the swamps, and the dead trees.

"They were now in the last dance, and appeared to have gone mad, and when at last the orchestra stopped, and Dick White doffed his cap with the indispensable flourish, and the moon shone on his bald scalp as he offered his arm to the fair one at his side, preparatory to leading her to a seat on the log, I fairly screamed with laughter, and then, to see that modest young lady suddenly throw out one of her number eleven boots, and her sledgehammer arm, and place Dick in an instant on his back and to observe the lady dancing a jig around him, yelling at the same time that made the distant hills echo, was glorious fun."

In this way Rylatt and his friends by temporary madness saved themselves from a larger insanity.

The next day Rylatt got three letters from his wife. The last was written by a neighbour because she was too ill to hold a pen. "Oh, Bob, come home," she wrote, "I can't bear it!" But he couldn't go home. He had a two-year contract with Moberly, and Moberly wouldn't release him. As the fall rains began, pouring down in such sheets that they couldn't prepare a hot meal, the party moved north again.

The whole valley was like a lake. Rylatt's clothing was drenched every night. He took it off, wrung it out, and then went to bed in soaking wet blankets. The following morning he put on his wet clothing again, shivering all over, his teeth chattering, as he realized how difficult it was going to be to make breakfast. Warm breakfasts were impossible. All they got were flapjacks covered with bacon grease and a muddy coffee made from beans placed in a piece of canvas and bruised between two rocks.

Now, with winter setting in and their goods and supplies far behind, they found themselves in the heart of the Rockies, 6,500 feet (1,980 m) above sea level, fifty miles (80 km) from their wintering place, "where no trail exists, nor ever has existed."

The country was totally unexplored. Every mile was a

Robert Rylatt and Henry Baird say good-bye to their workmates and guides.

horror. There were swamps to be crossed, heavy timber to be hacked through, and dense undergrowth to be chopped off so the animals could make it.

For weeks there was no scrap of news. But then on October 19 the pack train arrived and Rylatt was handed a slip of paper on which was scribbled the message he'd been dreading:

"Dear Rylatt – the papers state your wife has passed beyond the stream of time. Don't be cut up, dear old fellow."

There were no details. Three days later, brooding in his

tent, Rylatt was startled by a strange cry. His faithful dog, Nip, who had shared all his hardships, his blankets, and his food, had broken through the shore ice and was struggling vainly in the river. Rylatt tried to save him but failed. "Oh, God," he cried in his distress, "must everything be taken from me?"

And so the winter passed. By April Rylatt was nearly dead of scurvy, a disease caused primarily by the lack of dietary vitamin C. His mouth was in a dreadful state, the gums black, the teeth loose. In fact the gums swelled so badly at times they almost covered his teeth. It was impossible for him to chew anything, and he had to bolt his food without chewing. His legs had become black below the knee. His breath was sour and he was troubled with a dry cough. "I feel like an old man," he wrote.

Finally he talked Moberly into allowing him to quit the service and go home. And so, on the evening of May 13, 1873, he said his goodbyes. It was a bittersweet leave-taking. Suddenly he felt a pang of regret after having to turn his back on his comrades. They crowded around him with warm handshakes, and clumsy words of farewell. The cook made some doughnuts especially for the occasion. These men had been together for two years – and they had come to know one another as men only can under conditions of hardship and stress.

Rylatt set off with one companion, a burly Scot named Henry Baird. They took three horses and headed south towards Kamloops, through unknown country. They trudged through soaking moss, "so deep an animal could be buried overhead and suffocate." They swam and reswam the ice-cold rivers, pack horses and all. They crawled on their hands and knees across fallen timber. They stamped out a trail through the crust of melting snow. They foundered in the rapids of the treacherous rivers and they slashed away at the underbrush, whipping their animals unmercifully as they struggled on in search of feed for them.

A month went by. They were still on the trail. Their provisions were lost, their matches were almost gone, their sugar was used up, and all they had between them and starvation was a single sack of flour. Kamloops was still 150 miles (240 km) away.

At this point they came upon a meadow where the horses could graze. And so they made a fire, dried their clothing, and cooked some pancakes. Then they stretched out before the blaze – the closest thing to comfort they'd known for many weeks.

And here these two exhausted weather-beaten men fell to thinking about the future Canadian Pacific Railway. In their mind's eye they could see a train of cars sweeping along the flat, over the fierce streams, puffing and snorting at the mountains, and shrieking wildly, as some beast of the forest, scared at the new puffing monster, scurried off.

They talked about the passengers looking with weary eyes, hoping for the end of the route. They could almost see these travellers settling back in their corners in the parlour car, yawning, and complaining of tiredness, and dozing.

Then their thoughts turned to the dining car. And these

two hungry men began to describe the kind of dinner that might be served on such a train in the future: "Hot joints, mealy potatoes, pies, cheese, etc., and wine to be had for the paying for."

The fantasy grew. They began to think about the imaginary passengers, and the imaginary train. They pretended these passengers were looking out the train gazing on *them*, and remarking, "Those two fellows yonder seem to have it pretty much to themselves, as they toast their skins … and are doubtless happier and more at freedom than we…."

Finally the train of imagination rolled on beyond the forested horizon. Rylatt and Baird roused themselves, and counted their matches. They realized there would not be many more hot meals. They still had a long way to go, but the end of that long sentence in the Canadian Pacific Survey was at last in sight.

They cooked some more flapjacks on what was left of the fire – they would eat them cold on the following day. They saved what little tea and tobacco was left for an emergency. Then, wearily, they picked up their loads, gathered their grazing horses, and with that strange vision of the future still fresh in their minds set off once again into reality.

CHAPTER SIX

~

"That old devil," Marcus Smith

By the fall of 1872, Sandford Fleming had lost all confidence in Walter Moberly. He sent an Indian runner to the Moberly party, with a message ordering Moberly back to Kamloops. He said he had changed his mind about the surveys of the line. Moberly was to place the supplies and pack animals in the charge of another man.

Fleming believed this raw tactic would force Moberly to quit the service. But Moberly stubbornly decided to ignore the order and press on with a survey of the Yellow Head, come hell or blizzard. He felt "the instructions conveyed in the letter were too childish to be followed." He carried on the work anyway, according to his own best judgment and would only obey orders "when I could see they were sensible, but not otherwise." Moberly said he went into the service "for business, not to be made a fool of."

Fleming tried again after the New Year, 1873. He sent another message by a Métis runner, telling Moberly that a new man, Marcus Smith, had taken over. Smith, who had been in charge of a party exploring the Homathco River in

1872 while Moberly was at Howse, would now be in charge of *all* surveys in British Columbia. He would, in short, be Moberly's boss. This did not sit well with Moberly.

He did some work for Smith who wanted to find out if there was a pass that could be used up the North Thompson River. Moberly reported "an impenetrable wall of rock, snow and ice." Then, finally, he did quit.

Moberly left for Ottawa where he had a chilly meeting with Fleming. He hung around the capital waiting for the engineer-in-chief to sign his expense accounts. Fleming turned down the first one and then had a second auditor go over Moberly's bill again. Finally he passed the expenses, but Moberly had waited so long that he was forced to borrow money to pay for his room and board.

Moberly left British Columbia and moved to Winnipeg where he got a job building the city's first sewers. For the rest of his life he complained bitterly about the way Fleming had treated him. Eventually, the railway *would* go south, but not through Moberly's favourite pass – the Howse. The railway builders discarded it – as they discarded the Yellow Head – in favour of the Kicking Horse.

There was one triumph, however, of which Walter Moberly could not be cheated. Twenty years after he discovered the Eagle Pass, the last spike of the Canadian Pacific Railway would be driven at Craigellachie. It was a significant spot, though not everybody realized it. For it was there that Moberly had stood and, in that mystical moment, had chalked on a blazed tree his prophecy that the overland railway would have to come this way.

Marcus Smith, the surveyor who replaced Moberly, was undoubtedly the most controversial figure the Canadian Pacific Survey produced. No two men seemed to agree about him. Moberly liked him. Another called him "a wonderful man to my mind." A third mentioned "the fire and sparkle of Marcus Smith's genius." But somebody else said he was "a very crabbed and impatient man, though withal very kind of heart."

Some of those who worked under him used harsher terms. Rylatt, when he was at a low point on the Columbia, wrote in a fury that "Smith was a hard, unjust, and arbitrary wretch." In the summer of 1872, a young surveyor named Edgar Fawcett, toiling in the Homathco country, called him "an old devil" and wrote in his diary, "I did not come here to be blackguarded by Mr. Smith for forty-five dollars a month." And when Smith announced he was leaving the party and moving on, another member wrote in his diary that it was "the best news we have heard since we left Victoria."

Smith was a pretty good hater himself. He called one man "a Yankee sneak," and another "a little toady." The man who replaced Sandford Fleming, Collingwood Schreiber, "was mean and unfair," in Smith's mind. Another was "a thorough fraud," and a third "a crazy conceited fellow."

Smith was suspicious of all politicians. He thought that Alexander Mackenzie, the prime minister who followed John A. Macdonald, was dishonest. He suspected the Governor General, Lord Dufferin, of speculating in railway lands. As for Macdonald himself, he would "sacrifice any-thing or anybody to smooth down difficulties."

This gives you a pretty good idea of the tensions that existed among men who are driven hard in the far corners of the country. But Smith was special. Like Moberly who wanted the Howse Pass, and Fleming who wanted the Yellow Head Pass, Smith had his own route to the Pacific and he bitterly opposed anybody who dared to disagree.

Smith's route led through the Pine Pass, which is well to the north of the Yellow Head, and then southwest through Fort George, in the heart of British Columbia, across the Chilcoten plains to the headwaters of the Homathco River and thence down that turbulent river to its mouth at Bute Inlet on the Pacific.

Smith quarrelled with anyone who favoured any other line. He fought with Fleming because Fleming wanted to go through the Yellow Head and down the Fraser River to Burrard Inlet (the present site of Vancouver). He fought with his colleague, Henry Cambie, because Cambie wanted to take the railroad through to Port Simpson on the Pacific Ocean well to the north. He also fought with Alexander Mackenzie, who was both prime minister and minister of public works. In fact, he even refused to speak to him because Mackenzie dared to argue with him.

He used every trick he knew to force the government to accept his Pine Pass-Bute Inlet route. He wrote to members of parliament. He sent secret surveys into the north. He arranged for letters and articles to appear in the newspapers. He bombarded everybody with his views.

He was darkly suspicious of conspiracies. He believed his reports were being suppressed out of jealousy. He blamed Fleming for that. Fleming, a mild man, bore it all calmly.

But Fleming did his best to get rid of Smith. In fact, he thought at one point that he had fired him. But Smith stuck around. Fleming then acted as if Smith didn't exist. But Smith was a born survivor. And he wasn't fired.

Smith was entranced by the long fiord of Bute Inlet, which led to the turbulent Homathco. "A scene of gloomy grandeur, probably not met with in any other part of the world," he called it. It was, in short, love at first sight as it had been with Moberly and the Howse Pass.

Most surveyors' diaries are pretty blunt. A tired man, squatting at the edge of a river bank, scribbling with a stub of pencil and greasy notebook, doesn't generally wax poetic; but Smith did. He had a habit of noting curious things around him – the character of Indian communities, for instance, or the spectacle of a young native girl throwing off her clothes and bathing in the river. Sometimes he was positively lyrical about his favourite region:

"Scene awfully grand – the river rushing and foaming in a narrow chain between walls of rock, a frowning cliff overhanging all, and the snow-capped mountains piercing clouds and hidden by curtains of glaciers glittering blue and cold in the sunlight." That isn't the way most surveyors wrote.

Later on he wrote for an official government report an equally poetic description of the Chilcoten meadows – "the silence of the plains only broken by the silent tread of the Indian or the sad wail of the solitary loon." Of his favourite canyon, the Homathco, he wrote, "The awful grandeur of the mountains, the roar of the waters, and the constant sense of danger kept the nerves strong and the mind active."

His description of the "charming" mile-wide valleys of the Chilcoten and Chilanko Rivers sounded like that of a lovelorn suitor composing a tribute to his girlfriend. Smith wrote of bottom lands, ripe and mellow with bunch growth, with clear streams winding through them in graceful curves, of the pale, greyish-green of the grasses "in agreeable harmony with the dark foliage of the spruce," and of the "picturesque irregularity of the evergreens … the whole forming a scene of pristine beauty rarely to be met with." Compared to the routine language of some of his colleagues, Smith's seemed almost sensual.

He had just turned fifty-six – a stubby man with a barrel chest, as tough as leather and bristly as a wart hog. His hooded eyes, drooping moustache, and grizzled beard gave him an almost sour look. Born in the English county of Northumberland, he'd been a land surveyor all his life, first in England and Wales, then in South Africa, and since 1850 in Canada.

Like so many of the other surveyors – men accustomed to fending for themselves in severe climates – he was totally self-confident and more than a little proud.

"I have no claim for genius," he wrote at the close of his career (he lived to be eighty-nine), "but a strong love of my profession, and an aptitude and energy of carrying out great works, and a determination for honesty and accuracy for which I have so far carried out, that in long practice there has never been a dollar lost to any of my employers from any blunder of mine."

He was a hard drinker. In the so-called dry areas, he carried a keg of "lime juice" which really contained whisky. He wasn't an easy man to work with, for he didn't allow incompetence or fatigue or indeed any kind of human frailty. One of his employees, Edgar Fawcett, was toiling up a steep, rocky hill in June 1872, when a huge boulder bounced down the slope and struck him a blow that knocked him out. Smith was infuriated. He said he couldn't have children working for him. "That boy who could not keep out of the way of stones would have to be sent home," he said.

He was distressed by anything that delayed the survey. He expected his men to be as tough as he was. As George Hargreaves, one of the levellers in his party, wrote in his diary in June of 1872, "Sunday morning and no one sorry for it except perhaps old Smith, who I think would like to keep everyone at work night and day and then growl and snap at anyone who came near or happened to speak to him."

Three days later he wrote that "Old Smith came to camp about 7:30 and boiled over, accusing us of putting obstacles in his way and saying he would carry through the survey if he had to send five thousand miles for men."

Six days later: "Had a row with Old Smith for not

bringing the levels through before stopping work.... Says he, 'what did you mean by saying you was through, you must be an idiot.'"

Two days after that: "It appears Smith had a big row with two or three of the men and also with Bristow, the Transit. Called him a Gd-dmd fool and Idiot, who said he would not have such language used to him, that he would go home to Canada if he continued to use it, and also told Smith he was stopping the work by carrying on so. Smith told him to go back to his instrument or he would give him the Gd damdist daming ever he had dam'd...."

Young Fawcett's diary also reveals his feelings about Smith: "It was most awful the way that old devil swore and went on generally," he wrote a week after the incident with the boulder. "He swore at me for the most ordinary things and kept us from dinner until half-past two."

Smith certainly made no distinctions. He barked equally at transit men, levellers, axemen, and Indian packers with a fine democracy. But the Indians weren't going to take any of Smith's insults. They simply unloaded their canoes and prepared to head off into the wilderness.

Smith called in Hargreaves and asked him who had authorized the Indians to leave. Hargreaves replied the Indians didn't require any authorization to do anything.

That remark seemed to astonish Smith. "He said we must talk about that," Hargreaves wrote, "only while he was talking about it, they were going, which put him in a flutter rather."

Smith asked what the Indians wanted. The Indians

replied they didn't want to work for him. Hargreaves stopped a mass walkout by apologizing on Smith's behalf and agreeing to pay the Indians in cash at the time of every trip.

But if Smith was hard on the others, he was also hard on himself. When he was sixty years of age, he travelled for one thousand miles (1,600 km) through the Lake Superior country by canoe, all in a single summer, making two hundred portages that varied from a few yards to four miles (6.4 km).

Young chainmen and their rodmen who worked for him must have seen him as a superman, although a satanic one. At the end of each day they were so thoroughly exhausted they were prepared to throw in the sponge. Some of their diary excerpts from the Bute Inlet survey of 1872, when Smith was driving his men without mercy, give an idea of how hard the job was:

"So tired I could hardly drag myself along. After one of the hardest, hottest and longest days I had ever experienced in my life, we arrived at 'W' camp. I was so far done in I could not get up and sat down to rest."

"Yesterday I really thought I should have to give in I felt so the loss of having eaten nothing all day but a bit of bread and fat pork in 12 hours. If this is surveying, I have had my bellyful of it."

"I am heartily sick of the whole business and feel like turning tail."

" … legs and feet all benumbed and aching fearfully. I felt like giving up and leaving it many times but knowing it

Marcus Smith and his horse get caught in a swamp.

had to be done sometime, and if we left it today would have to go again tomorrow, managed to get through...."

It must have galled these younger men that the demonic Smith, a man twice their age, was driving hard late into the evening, scaling the rocks and forging through the icy waters with enough breath left in his barrel chest to fling curses upon the stragglers.

Actually, his own diary reveals he was as exhausted as any. He "felt terribly used up," he wrote on July 9, 1872 – a phrase that keeps recurring on those cramped pages. But he would not give up. That night, used up or not, he had to work out the calculations of his travels across the mountains.

Four days after that when he finally boarded the boat to Victoria, to the immense relief of his men, he was close to collapse. "Fatigue set in after a month of excessive labour and anxiety, and I lay and dozed the hours away, totally unfit for anything."

Yet, sick or not, Smith was back in the same country a month later. He was tortured by pains and cramps in his hip and his left leg. By August 11 he was so ill he couldn't get out of bed until noon. But he did get up. He threw a saddle on his horse and headed off across a swamp – a swamp so bad that he had to leave it and make his way up the side of a hill, still on horseback.

After that detour, he plunged into another swamp. This time the horse was caught in the mud. Smith tried to spur it on but the saddle slipped off and he tumbled in. He was too weak to put the saddle back on his horse, and yet he managed to crawl all the way to the head of the lake, where he found two Indians who looked after him.

He was still at it in the same country in the summer of 1875. By then he was in his sixtieth year. He confided to a friend that he had "less heart for that journey than any I have undertaken. I am far from well and very weak, and the mountain torrents are very high."

When Smith wrote that letter, he was planning to force his way from the Chilcoten plains through the Cascade Mountains by way of the Homathco Pass and down to Bute Inlet. He set off on foot with five Lillooet Indians and a Chilcoten guide, struggling for two and a half days along the dripping cliffs of the canyons. It often took him several hours to move a few yards, because the party had to climb as high as fifteen hundred feet (457 m), and climb down again to get around the spurs of rocks that jutted from the face of the canyon wall.

At one point, Smith found he couldn't bridge a torrent. Six of the largest trees, which they had thrown across the chasm, had been swept away like so many chips. He and his men were forced to detour by way of a glacier, fifteen miles (24 km) long, whose sharp ridges they crossed on their hands and knees. That was not the kind of summer excursion that any doctor would prescribe for a sick man in his sixtieth year.

En route to the coast, Smith discovered the bridges that had been built for him had been swept away by the mountain torrents. It took him and his men seven hours to build an Indian fly bridge over the Grand Canyon of the Homathco. He said it "looked like a fishing rod and line hanging over the torrent, the butt end resting on the ground and loaded with boulders." He tested it himself, creeping out over it, then dropping heavily to the rocks below. It took him six hours, scrambling over tangled creepers, huge deadfalls, and masses of detached rocks, to reach camp.

Smith's love-hate relationship with this strangely haunting land of grim canyons and smiling meadows had, to borrow his own phrase, used him up. Would all his work be in vain? Survey parties were crawling over the rumpled face of British Columbia and probing the ragged fiords of the coastline, seeking the best method of reaching the Pacific by railway. Sandford Fleming was considering no fewer than eleven different routes, leading down the mountain spine to salt water. Only two led through Smith's country.

What if another route should be chosen? What if all those ghastly days in the numbing bogs and among the brooding crags should end in defeat? But Marcus Smith was not a man to contemplate defeat. And he not yet begun to fight.

CHAPTER SEVEN

~

The Battle of the Routes

THEY CALLED IT THE "Battle of the Routes." Everybody, it seemed – politicians as well as surveyors – had their own favourite route. And each had his own reasons why "his" route through the mountains and down to the seacoast should be chosen. All the routes led out of Fort Saskatchewan not far from Fort Edmonton. But from Edmonton there were seven possible ways for the railway to reach the ocean.

As far as British Columbia was concerned, there were only two routes that really mattered. One was the ancient trail used by the fur traders and explorers through the Yellow Head Pass and down the Fraser canyon to Burrard Inlet. If chosen, it could guarantee the prosperity of the interior cities – Kamloops, Yale, and New Westminster and all the valley points between. This was the route for which mainland B.C. was prepared to fight.

The other route would probably lead from the Yellow Head through the Cariboo country and the Chilcoten plains to Marcus Smith's favourite river, the Homathco, and then on to Bute Inlet. At that point it would leap the straits to Nanaimo, and thence to Victoria. It would guarantee the prosperity of the dying Cariboo gold region, and also of Vancouver Island. And so, the city of Victoria on Vancouver Island, and New Westminster on the mainland, together with the interior towns, fought the Battle of the Routes.

By 1877 the battle had reached the stage of a pamphlet war – the tried and true technique of those days. Print and paper were cheap. Pamphlets could be issued as swiftly as a newspaper. Supporters of burning causes fought each other with words as in earlier times they had duelled with swords. So in the Battle of the Routes the opponents attacked each other with blizzards of paper.

By 1877, Fleming, who favoured the Yellow Head Pass, was unable to make up his mind on the best way to the Pacific. By 1875 there was general understanding that Bute Inlet would be the terminus. But in 1876, Fleming decided, a bit late, that he ought to ask the Royal Navy its opinion of the various harbours along the coast. The overwhelming opinion, to his surprise, was in favour of Burrard Inlet, not Bute.

Fleming was walking a difficult line. He knew that whichever route was chosen he would be attacked by the supporters of the other one. But he had an alternative idea. He pointed out that the harbour at the mouth of the Skeena River, near present-day Prince Rupert, was five hundred miles (800 km) closer to the Orient than the other two. The

Navy dismissed that as "totally unfit for the Ocean Terminus." But Fleming refused to rule it out.

Then in 1876, Fleming's doctor ordered a complete rest. The Battle of the Routes had unnerved him. Marcus Smith took over temporarily in his place. For nineteen months between the spring of 1876 and 1878, he was in charge.

Of course, Smith wouldn't give up Bute Inlet, which he had surveyed with such enthusiasm. Actually the route that he chose was totally impractical. There wasn't room to build a city as a terminus for the railway in the narrow confines of the inlet. Also the rails would have to cross the ocean to Vancouver Island, leaping by causeway from island to island – no fewer than seven islands – at an enormous cost and some danger, since the waters were treacherous.

But Marcus Smith was adamant. In his view the railway would not only go through Bute Inlet, it would cross the Rockies – not at Sandford Fleming's favourite pass, the Yellow Head, but by the Pine Pass, five hundred miles (800 km) to the north. He decided to send a survey party to the Pine River country on a completely confidential trip. And he went out to British Columbia himself, to return full of enthusiasm for the Peace River country.

He speeded up his behind-the-scenes work to get his route approved. He told his assistant, Joseph Hunter, to leak some information to the press about his Pine Pass explorations, but to make sure it wasn't official. Then he told Hunter to allow himself to be pumped by reporters into praising the country he had explored. Meanwhile,

Smith issued a anonymous press release, which began, "Not withstanding that the matter has been kept very quiet, it has leaked out that the explorations of the acting Engineer-in-Chief Marcus Smith, from the East, and Mr. Hunter, from the West, last summer have been most successful." The press release praised the Pine Pass/Bute Inlet route.

Smith saw dark plots and sinister motives everywhere. He lived in a cloak-and-dagger world of the mind, in which he imagined himself desperately fighting off, at great personal and financial risk, the dark forces of treason and corruption. For he believed so strongly in his own route that it did not occur to him that anybody could advocate another route without being crooked.

Meanwhile he was up against the new prime minister, Alexander Mackenzie, who favoured the Burrard route. In order to get his way, the prime minister actually had to get around his own acting engineer-in-chief.

There were many reasons why Mackenzie wanted to go by way of Burrard Inlet. One was the Navy report, which favoured it. Another was the strong urging of several mainland members of Parliament. The Governor General himself had been out west and thought the Burrard Inlet was the best. New surveys by Henry Cambie, ordered by Mackenzie himself (without Smith's knowledge), had also suggested the Burrard route. And finally, there was Smith's bullheadedness. He had got the prime minister's back up. By March 1878, Mackenzie had ceased to consult him or even speak to him.

Meanwhile, Smith continued to press for the Bute Inlet route. He suggested another year's delay to settle the final location of the line. That presented the prime minister with a problem. He could scarcely settle on Burrard Inlet in the face of the direct and public opposition of his acting chief engineer. The islanders in Victoria would pounce on that, and cry foul. He had only one choice. Without telling Marcus Smith, he sent for Sandford Fleming, who found his sick leave in England interrupted.

Fleming found his department in an uproar. Smith had stated in public that some of his people were working secretly with railway contractors – a charge designed to anger the members of that proud service. An unholy row followed. Smith told Fleming he no longer had confidence in him. He said Fleming must no longer consider him, Smith, a member of the department. As Fleming later put it, "he did not receive his dismissal, but he was as good as dismissed and I was not at liberty to consult him any longer, inasmuch as he was no longer a public officer."

Obviously he expected Smith to quit, as he had expected Moberly to quit, but Smith hung on – as he had once hung on to the slippery crags of the Homathco canyon. Meanwhile, Fleming was finally convinced that if engineering decisions alone were to govern the selection of a route, and if that selection couldn't be postponed further, then the Bute Inlet route should rejected, and the Burrard Inlet route selected.

And that was that. On July 12, 1878, the government

settled officially on the Fraser River/Burrard Inlet route, and prepared to call for tenders for the building of the railway through the Fraser River.

This meant that a new city – Vancouver – would spring up on Burrard Inlet. But that was several years in the future. Before that happened, Fleming's favourite route through the Yellow Head Pass would also be rejected by the new company organized to build the Canadian Pacific Railway.

The railway would not go through the Pine Pass, or the Yellow Head Pass, or the Howse Pass, or any of the other passes that had been located through the mountains by dedicated men, working under impossible conditions. In the end the railway would be taken far to the south, through the Kicking Horse Pass, the closest to the American border. That meant that other men would have to run survey lines through the three ranges of mountains that blocked the way to the seacoast. These would not be members of the Canadian Pacific Survey; they would be new surveyors working for a private company. But that is another story.

Index

Also Available

THE MEN IN SHEEPSKIN COATS

As the nineteenth century gave way to the twentieth, the Canadian West experienced an unprecedented wave of immigration and settlement. Many of these homesteaders were "the men in sheepskin coats" and their families – natives of eastern Europe who had left their impoverished, crowded homelands for what they hoped would be a better life.

At first they were not welcomed with open arms. Politicians and newspaper writers spoke of them as "foreign trash." Gradually, however, these hard-working immigrants came to be seen as essential to Canadian prosperity and the idea of the Canadian mosaic.

In this second instalment of *Canada Moves West*, Pierre Berton vividly captures the hardships and triumphs of Canada's Slavic settlers as they struggle to find "a place in the sun" in the vastness of the West.